3/184/18

INSECTS

THE MOST FUN BUG BOOK EVER

SNEED B. COLLARD III

Charlesbridge

Six-Legged Thanks

This book would not have molted into adulthood without the help of some very special people. First off, I'd like to thank my family, who always helps me see more of nature and fuels my eagerness for discovery. I'd also like to thank Randi Rivers, who gave me excellent guidance on early drafts of the book—and threw in a few insect jokes to boot! Big thanks to Yolanda Scott for her enthusiasm in making this book come alive, and to my editor, Julie Bliven, for guiding this work through its step-by-step metamorphosis! Finally, I'd like to thank my son, Braden Collard, for using his considerable artistic talent to create an insect up-close and personal!

cover: dragonfly larva

page 1: grasshopper, Malaysia

page 2: treehopper, Costa Rica

above: clearwing butterflies, Costa Rica

page 5: cicadas, Costa Rica

To my friend Larry Pringle,
who takes time to search for cicadas
and marvel at monarchs

Copyright © 2017 by Sneed B. Collard III
All rights reserved, including the right of reproduction in whole or in part in any form. Charlesbridge and colophon are registered trademarks of Charlesbridge Publishing, Inc.

Published by Charlesbridge
85 Main Street, Watertown, MA 02472
(617) 926-0329
www.charlesbridge.com

Library of Congress Cataloging-in-Publication Data
Names: Collard, Sneed B., III, author.
Title: Insects: the most fun bug book ever / Sneed B. Collard III.
Description: Watertown, MA : Charlesbridge, [2017] | Description based on print version record and CIP data provided by publisher; resource not viewed.
Identifiers: LCCN 2015050153 (print) |
LCCN 2015043919 (ebook) |
ISBN 9781607349334 (ebook) |
ISBN 9781607349341 (ebook pdf) |
ISBN 9781580896429 (reinforced for library use)
Subjects: LCSH: Insects—Miscellanea—Juvenile literature. | Insects as pets—Juvenile literature. Classification: LCC QL467.2 (print) | LCC QL467.2 .C657 2017 (ebook) | DDC 595.7—dc23
LC record available at http://lccn.loc.gov/2015050153

Printed in China
(hc) 10 9 8 7 6 5 4 3 2 1

Display type set in Animated Gothic by Bob Alonso
Text type set in Adobe Caslon by Adobe Systems Incorporated
Color separations by Colourscan Print Co Pte Ltd, Singapore
Printed by 1010 Printing International Limited in Huizhou, Guangdong, China
Production supervision by Brian G. Walker
Designed by Susan Mallory Sherman and Diane M. Earley

All photographs courtesy of Sneed B. Collard III, with the exception of the following:
© Vitalii Hulai/Shutterstock.com, (/gallery-1270564p1.html), jacket image
© Braden Collard, p. 10
© Ritfuse/Shutterstock.com, p. 22
© Stacey Ann Alberts/Shutterstock.com, p. 27

Table of Contents

he Earth According to Insects

Planet Earth is a decent place for us mammals to live. Fish, reptiles, and birds do pretty well here, too. But if you look at all the animals on our planet, one thing becomes clear: while Earth is a good place for many kinds of critters, it is absolutely great for one particular group of animals—INSECTS!

Don't believe me? Check out the chart to the right.

Did you notice anything unusual? No, not our human devotion to superheroes. I'm talking about the humongous number of insect species—close to *one million*! What's more, scientists haven't even come close to counting them all. Scientists guess that the true number of insect species on our planet lies between two million and thirty million—yes, thirty MILLION! In other words, most of the animals on Earth are insects.

How is that possible?

opposite: Weaver ants form living chains to pull leaves and then stitch them together into a temporary shelter, using sticky silk from their larvae.

Animal group	Approximate number of species identified so far
Mammals	5,400
Birds	10,600
Reptiles	10,300
Comic-book superheroes	1,000+
Amphibians	7,500
Fish	33,200
Arachnids (spiders, scorpions, mites, ticks)	60,000+
Insects	**950,000+**

These numbers reflect only the species that have been discovered and described by scientists. The numbers are constantly changing as scientists find new species—and writers create new comic book superheroes!

Wings and a close relationship with plants have helped this black swallowtail butterfly and other insects dominate our planet.

Insects have three major advantages over most other animals. The first is that they got an early start. According to the most recent studies, insects appeared on Earth about 480 million years ago. That's about 160 million years before the first reptiles and almost *300 million years* before the first mammals. That gave insects a lot of time to eat doughnuts and drink their morning coffee before animals like humans and bears came along. It also meant insects had much more time to evolve into different species.

Insects were also the first animals to fly. That helped them reach most places on the planet. One thing all those places had in common was plants—and gee, do you think insects took advantage of this plentiful food source? You bet your stinky sneakers they did. Feeding on and living with plants has been key to insects' success. Without plants, many insects would be without food or shelter.

Finally, take a look at an insect's body—especially that exoskeleton, or hard external shell. This tough shell consists of chitin, a substance similar to the keratin in your fingernails. Chitin exoskeletons protect insects while keeping them from drying out. They allow insects to live in some of the world's harshest environments. They also make it awfully hard to *squish* insects. Ounce for ounce, insects are about the toughest animals anywhere.

All these factors have helped make insects *the* dominant life-form on Earth today. So why do many of us think about insects only when a fly is buzzing around our corn dog or when our kid sister is stung by a bee? I don't know, but I'm going to try to change that. By the end of this book, I want you bowing down to the true rulers of our planet—or at least shouting, "Righteous exoskeleton, dude!" the next time you pass an insect on the street.

Let's start by taking a closer look at an insect's awesome construction . . .

This bizarre cricket from Costa Rica shows the three different sections of an insect's body and the tough exoskeleton that is a key to insect survival.

Designed to Dominate

Insects did not take over the world because of their blazing intelligence. The pinhead-sized brain of an insect does what it needs to do, but even the smartest insect won't outscore you on the class spelling bee. What *has* allowed insects to take over the world is the toughest, most adaptable body plan imaginable.

This "professionally rendered" bee drawing illustrates an insect's basic body plan.

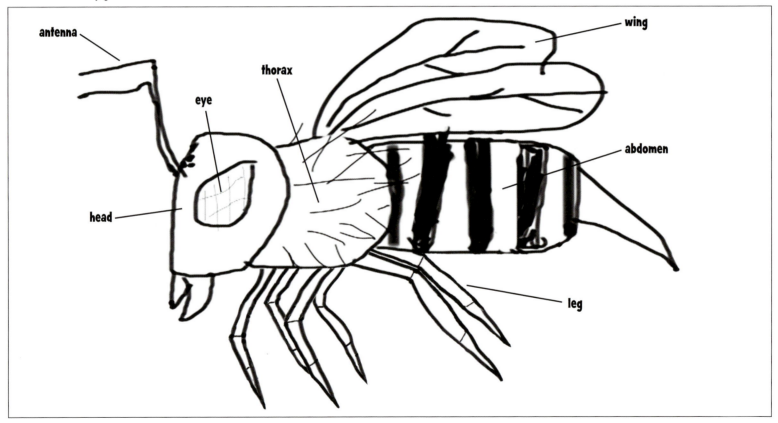

antenna

wing

thorax

eye

abdomen

head

leg

The Head

Insects come with three—count 'em, *three*—sections: the head, the thorax, and the abdomen. The head bristles with navigational and sensory equipment. See those two big eyes? They're not like yours and mine. Each eye is called a compound eye and contains many little units called ommatidia. Each ommatidium acts as a single eye—but unlike a human eye, it captures only the portion of the scene on which it is focused. Some insects have a few hundred ommatidia, while others have thousands. An insect's brain—also located in the head—takes information from these units to form pictures of the world.

Two antennae poke out of almost every insect's head. Antennae come in many shapes and sizes and, boy, do they do a lot of work!

How Well Can an Insect See?

Scientists calculate that human eyes form a sharper picture of an object than insect eyes do. Insect eyes, though, detect movement much more quickly than ours do. This helps insects chase down their prey—and avoid flyswatters.

Like us, insects can see color. It's no accident that many flowers have bright, showy colors. Flowers are giant billboards that tell butterflies and bees, "Hey, come pollinate me!" Insects can also see ultraviolet light, which humans cannot see. This probably helps them navigate during the daytime. Seeing ultraviolet light also gives them a lot of information about the world that we humans are just beginning to understand.

Besides having well-equipped heads, walking sticks, or "stick bugs," grow longer than any other insects. Some can reach one and a half feet long!

How Do Insects Breathe?

If you see an upset insect, don't tell it to take a deep breath. It can't! That's because insects don't have lungs. Instead, they have a system of tubes called trachea. Air enters the tracheae through openings called spiracles, which are located on the insect's exoskeleton, usually on the abdomen. Insects can open and close the spiracles to help keep their bodies from drying out. Once air enters the spiracles, it spreads to smaller and smaller tubes until it comes into contact with the insect's tissues and the cells that need it.

Some large insects use muscles to pump air in and out of their tracheae. In many small insects, air simply drifts in and out with the animals' movements. What about insects that live in the water? Water beetles have evolved special adaptations that allow them to stay underwater longer. Some carry a bubble of air underwater with them. In others, part of the exoskeleton has evolved to form a kind of gill that actually lets the animals breathe underwater.

With its antennae, an insect can detect movement, temperature, smell, sound, humidity, chemicals, and even which way its body is positioned. Antennae *cannot* pick up satellite TV or Wi-Fi, but still, don't you wish you had a pair?

One last thing you'll find on an insect's head is mouthparts. We all have mouthparts, of course, but an insect has several different sets, including the mandibles, maxillae, and labium. They are used to grab, bite, and chew food, but you'll discover later that mouthparts can also be used for sucking, piercing, or sponging up gross and disgusting liquids to eat.

The Thorax

The thorax, or the middle part, of an insect is its transportation center. Insect manufacturers always attach an insect's legs to its thorax. If you see an insect with legs on its head, *don't buy it!* Speaking of legs, all adult insects have six. Not two. Not four. Not eight. Six—otherwise it's not an insect. If an adult insect loses a leg, it can often grow a new one, but the animal may not be able to dance or juggle ant eggs for a while.

An insect's wings are also attached to the thorax. Most insects have two sets of wings, but some groups, such as flies, have only a single set. Over years of evolution, fleas, lice, springtails, and a few other insects have lost their wings altogether. These poor guys usually have to ride buses or take taxis to get around.

The bright abdomen of the polka-dot wasp moth—also called the oleander moth—warns potential predators that it could be poisonous and dangerous. In actuality, the moth is harmless.

The Abdomen

The abdomen, or hind part, of an insect is mostly used to store luggage. Or, more accurately, important insect anatomy! If you popped open an insect's abdomen, you would see parts of its digestive, circulatory, respiratory, and nervous systems. The abdomen also carries the most important part of an insect—its reproductive system.

Let's swarm in for a closer look at some especially amazing insects.

The Fastest and the Toughest

Although all insect bodies are impressive, some appear to push the limits of what's possible. Whether it's how well they fly or how tough they are, the fastest and the toughest insects are especially prepared for survival.

Built for Speed

Dragonflies and damselflies are the fighter jets of the insect world. Unlike the wings of most insects, each dragonfly wing can be moved independently. With these wings, dragonflies and damselflies hover, do loop-the-loops, and even fly

Many scientists consider dragonflies the best flyers nature has ever produced.

backward! One scientist called them the best fliers the planet has ever produced. And did I mention these insects are *fast*? Dragonflies accelerate quickly and have been clocked at more than thirty-five miles per hour. A few other insects, such as parasitic botflies, may fly faster, but who wants to hang out with a botfly that can lay its eggs in human flesh? Not me!

Of course, dragonflies and damselflies don't use their amazing flight skills to impress people at air shows. They use them to hunt and avoid predators. I once spent an entire hour watching damselflies pick off gnats above a creek at the bottom of the Grand Canyon. The damselflies were so skilled and quick that the gnats never stood a chance. Aren't you glad that you're not a gnat?

14

Ironclad beetles come equipped with impressive armor that protects them from enemies—and careless hikers.

Battle Ready

Over time, ironclad beetles have lost their ability to fly. Then again, who needs to fly when you're built like a tank? Ironclad beetles have some of the insect world's most impressive armor. How impressive? To mount dead specimens of ironclad beetles in their insect collections, scientists sometimes have to drill holes through the beetles' shells! That's what I call tough.

With their fearsome appearance, you'd think that ironclad beetles would attack villages and devour townspeople. You'd be wrong. Ironclad beetles eat fungus, and when they are attacked, they play dead. These animals are so tame that people sometimes glue decorations to the beetles and wear them as living jewelry. True story!

The forest of spines on saturniid moths provides a potent defense against most predators.

opposite: Many other species of caterpillars, including this caterpillar of the polka-dot wasp moth, also bristle with, well, *bristles*!

A Munchin' Machine!

Caterpillars may not look as tough as ironclad beetles, but don't underestimate them. As we all know, caterpillars are the larvae, or young stage, of moths and butterflies. The adult forms of these insects grab most of the television coverage, but caterpillars deserve their own fan clubs. Just look at those mouthparts! The mandibles of caterpillars are strong and tough—and they have to be to chow down leaves and other plant material. Caterpillars eat so much and so rapidly that they can destroy a farmer's crop faster than you can say, "Please don't burp at the table." In just twenty days, a tobacco hornworm caterpillar can increase its weight ten thousand times.

And did I mention a caterpillar's defenses? Birds have a special fondness for caterpillars, but caterpillars don't sit around waiting to get eaten. Many caterpillars are loaded with foul chemicals that make them taste bad. Others come equipped with fearsome—often poisonous—spines. Consider the giant caterpillar of this saturniid moth. Tropical birds called trogons have learned to knock the spines off by whacking the caterpillar against a branch. Other animals, though, might as well try eating a cactus.

Of course, being fast and tough isn't enough to keep all insects alive and thriving. To survive, insects have other incredible tools at their disposal. One of the most important is . . .

16

Chemical Communication

Communicating is an essential survival tool for most animals. Communicating helps animals warn each other about danger, frighten off an enemy, find a mate, and much more. With so many insects on Earth, it's not surprising that insects have come up with an astounding number of ways to talk to each other.

Crickets, grasshoppers, cicadas, and many other insects are famous for chirping—also called stridulation. They rub their legs or wings against hard little pads or bristles on their bodies to create a range of noises. The purpose of these noises is to attract mates or defend territories. Colors also help many insects warn or impress each other. But almost all insects have even more important communication technology—chemicals called pheromones.

Insects produce most pheromones themselves, but sometimes they steal them from other insects or foods that they eat. These chemicals have two functions. Some pheromones trigger physical changes in an insect. For instance, a caterpillar's metamorphosis into a butterfly is jump-started by the release of certain pheromones inside the animal's body. More on that later.

Insects rely on a second group of pheromones strictly for communication. Insect antennae have evolved to tell the difference between hundreds—maybe thousands—of different pheromones. Ants, for instance, are famous for leaving pheromone trails that lead the rest of the colony to food sources. Each ant's body leaves a bit of pheromone behind so that other ants know where to go. As one food supply dwindles, fewer ants follow that trail, and the pheromone evaporates. That way, ants follow only the strongest trails.

Chemical Downsides

The use of pheromones is not always a win-win situation for insects seeking mates. For example, many flowers produce "perfumes" that attract insects wishing to mate. Instead of getting to mate, though, the insects become delivery vans for the flower's pollen. And some sneaky spiders release female pheromones to attract male moths. The lovesick moths show up, only to become the spider's dinner. Humans have even developed bait traps filled with pheromone chemicals to catch and kill harmful insects.

These harvester ants lay down pheromone trails that help them find and transport food.

When they feel threatened, insects that feed or work in a group release alarm pheromones. These signal other insects to flee from or attack an intruder. If you've ever been stung by a swarm of bees or wasps, you have experienced this kind of pheromone in painful detail. Pheromones, though, play their most important role in mating—which brings us to the subject of . . .

Hatching the Family Unit

The larvae of these orange mating psyllid flies help control melaleuca trees that have invaded southern Florida. The larvae do this by sucking the juices from the leaves of the trees.

Making babies is every adult insect's ultimate goal in life. Insects don't wait until they graduate from college and find good jobs to start a family. Most adult insects have a life span of only a few days or weeks, so they must act quickly to ensure the survival of their species.

It is strange but true that some insects do not need to mate in order to reproduce. Small, sap-sucking insects called aphids are parthenogenetic. The female can start cranking out eggs or live babies all by herself, with no help from a male. To make a baby, however, most other insect species require a sperm from a male to fertilize an egg from a female.

Not surprisingly, insects have come up with an astounding variety of tricks and behaviors to find mates. As we already, *ahem*, heard, male crickets and cicadas perform beautiful songs to attract females. Many butterflies, flies, and beetles attract each other with colors or other visual signals. Male hangingflies and balloon flies capture another insect and then offer it to a female to eat—an insect's version of taking a girl out to dinner! However, the Number One Favorite Method for insects to attract the opposite sex is to release pheromones.

As we already talked about, pheromones tell insects all kinds of things about each other. They communicate whether an insect is a male or female, if it is ready to mate, and probably all kinds of things scientists haven't even discovered! What's more, insect species can detect pheromones from incredible distances using their supersensitive antennae. In one experiment, male luna moths successfully found a female six and a half miles away! With a range like that, who needs a cell phone?

Once they've found a mate, males usually transfer their sperm to females in tiny, little packets called spermatophores. Sometimes the male sets his spermatophore on the ground or on a leaf, where the female picks it up. In many other species, the male transfers the spermatophore directly into the female's body.

Unfortunately, insects will never top the World's Best Parents Ever list. While most insects lay their eggs in a relatively safe place where the larvae will find food once they hatch, that's about as much parental care as larvae receive. Once the eggs are laid, it's "*Hasta la vista,* babies." The adults usually wander off and die within a few days. The eggs are left to get eaten, dry out, die of disease, or perish in a dozen other gruesome ways. When an egg is fortunate enough to hatch, however, a young insect's journey truly begins.

Drilling for Success

A few insects have taken classes on good parenting. Treehoppers feed by drilling into plants to drink their juices. Unfortunately, treehopper larvae are not capable of drilling through bark themselves. Mom solves this problem by staying with her brood, protecting them from predators, and drilling feeding holes for the youngsters until they can do it for themselves.

Although these walking sticks and other insects excel at making babies, most insects make lousy parents.

21

Growing Up Insect

If you were an adult insect and saw one of your babies after it hatched, you would probably let out a bloodcurdling scream and shout, "OH MY GOSH! WHAT IS THAT HORRIBLE MONSTER?" That's because insect babies start their lives as bizarre-looking—and sometimes repulsive—larvae.

After forming a pupa, caterpillars go through metamorphosis to become butterflies.

Some larvae are miniature versions of adult insects, but most have completely different appearances and behaviors—a lot like teenagers, in fact. A dragonfly larva hatches in the water and looks like a little bug-eyed torpedo. With fearsome "spring-loaded" jaws, it's quick to devour fish, tadpoles, and other aquatic insects. As it grows, the larva molts, or sheds its exoskeleton, several times, gradually changing in appearance. Finally it climbs out of the water, molts one last time, and emerges as a beautiful, air-breathing adult dragonfly.

Like the dragonfly, almost all other insect larvae go through many stages on their way to becoming adults. In most insects, the last larval stage forms a pupa, which is a stage between the larva and the adult. Often, the pupa is wrapped in a case called a cocoon. Inside this cocoon the pupa undergoes a radical transformation into an adult. Butterflies are most famous for this. The caterpillar (larva) spins a cocoon around itself. A few weeks later, SHAZAM! Out pops a butterfly. The transformation of an insect larva to an adult is called metamorphosis, a big word that simply means "change."

Rise of the Locusts

Some members of the grasshopper family are famous for gathering into giant swarms, or "plagues." These swarms can consist of billions of insects that sweep over thousands of square miles, devouring every shred of vegetation in their path. In October 1988 a giant swarm of desert locusts even managed to cross the Atlantic Ocean from West Africa to the islands of the Caribbean! Desert locusts start out as ordinary grasshoppers and live a solitary existence. But when heavy rains lead to an abundance of food, these grasshoppers rapidly multiply. If a sudden drought then creates a food shortage, a chemical called serotonin triggers changes in the animals' bodies and behaviors—turning the grasshoppers into a marauding swarm of locusts on the hunt for food!

As adults, most insects spend their lives close to where they were born. Like rock stars on tour, though, some take part in spectacular migrations. Insects migrate both to find better food sources and to avoid harsh seasons. Monarchs, painted ladies, and many other butterflies journey hundreds or thousands of miles between feeding and breeding areas. Eurasian milkweed bugs prefer day-trips and may migrate only a couple hundred yards or so to their hibernation grounds. While hiking in winter, I've encountered groups of thousands of ladybird beetles resting among plants or rocks high in the mountains. These animals gather there to hibernate. Personally, I'd pick a beach resort in Mexico or Puerto Rico. After all, beach resorts are nice and warm and a most relaxing place to pig out! Which brings us to our next course . . .

Tasty Insect Foods

Describing what insects eat is easy. They eat *everything*. Different insects eat plant juices, leaves, flowers, pollen, nectar, and wood. Visit your local Insect Mart and you'll also see insects stocking up on fungus, meat, blood, garbage—even other insects.

Some insects are generalists. They devour just about anything they find. The common cockroach chows down on paper, bread, leather, fruit, glue, beer, book bindings, dead skin, soap, grease, and in a pinch, other cockroaches. And you wonder why these pests are so hard to get rid of!

Cockroaches are generalists. They can eat just about anything.

Most insects have more discriminating tastes and specialize in certain types of foods. Insect mouthparts have evolved into an astounding variety of food-getting tools. A mosquito's mouthparts act like little hypodermic needles that allow the insect to pierce an animal's skin and drink its blood. A butterfly's mouthparts have evolved into a long tube or straw that lets it suck up nectar, rotting fruit, and other foods. A housefly's mouthparts act like a sponge that sops up liquid food. The housefly often spits out digestive juices to first dissolve the food, then sponges it up. I'd think twice before sharing your milkshake with one.

Salt is a precious resource for most animals. Here, sulphur butterflies gather at a natural salt lick to add some spice to their lives.

25

Nightmare on Spider Street

Not long ago I looked down on my porch and saw one of my least favorite animals: a hobo spider. Hobo spiders are an invasive species. They hitchhiked here from Europe and spread through much of the United States, driving out native spiders and giving people nasty, venom-filled bites. Normally I step on hobo spiders, but I resisted squashing this one. Why? Because a wasp was dragging the spider across the porch. The wasp was only half the size of the spider, but it belonged to a large group of wasps called spider wasps.

Adult spider wasps feed on nectar, but the larvae like even tastier treats. When a female spider wasp is ready to lay an egg, she stings and paralyzes a large spider. The wasp drags the spider into a burrow and lays a single egg in the spider's living flesh. The egg hatches inside the spider, and the larva feeds on the spider's tissues. Eventually the larva eats enough to kill the spider. It forms a pupa and then hatches into an adult spider wasp, ready to mate and to terrorize other spiders.

This tarantula hawk is a spider wasp that hunts . . . you guessed it: tarantulas.

One of the most interesting—okay, *grossest*—eating habits occurs in a group of insects called dung beetles. More than six thousand species of dung beetles fly and crawl across our planet. They feed on one of the world's richest food sources—mammal poop. Sounds crazy, right? But mammal poop is loaded with undigested food, nutrients, water, and bacteria. By eating it, dung beetles have hit the nutritional mother lode.

It's no surprise that dung beetles began to evolve at about the same time as mammals appeared on Earth. Dung beetles have an excellent sense of smell, and their antennae can distinguish between different kinds of poop. Don't even *think* about feeding cattle dung to a beetle that prefers elephant dung. It will unfriend you on Facebook faster than you can say, "Poop."

To keep surviving, of course, these beetles—and all other insects—have to solve another major problem. They have to avoid *becoming* food for other hungry animals.

Dung beetles perform a valuable service for the planet by
eating millions of tons of poop left behind by mammals.

Determined Defenses

Here's a humbling fact: without insects, most of Earth's animals would starve. The majority of birds, mammals, reptiles, and spiders depend on insects for food. Even grizzly bears devour moths and ladybird beetles to build up fat supplies. As you might guess, insects aren't super excited about this situation. After all, you can't rule the world if you're dead! To keep from becoming a meal, many insects bite, fly, or run away. Some protect themselves with heavy armor or poisonous spines. Others have evolved more ingenious defenses.

Bright colors often warn other animals that insects are poisonous or could be dangerous.

Potent Poisons

Brightly colored insects are not competing in beauty contests. As we've already seen, some use colors to attract mates. For most others, bright colors send a warning. The yellow-and-black markings of bees and wasps signal that anything bothering them will receive a painful sting of venom. Other insects contain nasty chemicals inside their bodies that make them taste bad. The monarch butterfly is famous for this. Monarch larvae feed on milkweed plants. Chemicals from these plants stay in the animals' bodies through metamorphosis and make adult monarchs taste bad.

Many insects rely on camouflage to hide from predators or ambush prey. Can you find the walking stick insect blending in with this tree bark?

Birds and other predators quickly learn to recognize the butterflies' orange-and-black markings and leave them alone. Many other butterflies, moths, and beetles also flash striking colors that shout, "We are poisonous!"

Hide-and-Seek

Most of us have heard of camouflage. It's a combination of colors and markings that hides an animal against its background. Although predators use camouflage to ambush their prey, more often an animal's camouflage hides it from predators.

"I'd Like My Locusts Deep Fried, Please."

Very few Americans eat insects. We'll eat almost anything else, but for some reason the thought of eating an insect is enough to make us lose our "civilized" lunch of ground-up cow, deep-fried fungus, and pulverized plant roots. In other cultures, however, people eagerly devour locusts, beetle grubs (larvae), termites, ants, cicadas, and bee larvae. People fry or roast the insects or grind them into flour to make bread. A diet of insects is probably healthier than what we eat now. A typical hamburger contains about 18 percent protein and 18 percent fat. A cooked grasshopper contains 60 percent protein and only 6 percent fat! The only question is: would you like that fried grasshopper with or without onion rings?

Mimicry helps this katydid look like a leaf!

opposite: A second kind of mimicry helps the caterpillar of the tiger swallowtail butterfly look like a fearsome snake!

Mimicry, Part One

Don't confuse camouflage with another amazing insect defense: mimicry. Mimicry occurs when an animal's body looks like another object. For example, the wings of this katydid look like leaves that have had a big bite taken out of them. Insects are some of the world's greatest mimics. Like camouflage, mimicry helps them stay hidden from both predators and prey. But insects use another kind of mimicry, too.

Mimicry, Part Two

Instead of mimicking their surroundings, some insects mimic other insects. They do this because they are relentless copycats. Well, actually, the real reason they do this is to pretend that they are poisonous or dangerous—even when they're not. Many tropical butterflies are poisonous, but some nonpoisonous species have identical "warning colors" to keep predators from eating them. Look at the snake on the next page. Wait a minute . . . that's not a snake! It's a caterpillar that looks like a snake. Do you think a bird might think twice before attacking it?

Of course, some kinds of insects don't have to worry about defending themselves as much as others do. Sure, these insects might bite or sting, but they can also use sheer numbers to overwhelm predators. Scientists call these animals "social insects." I call them . . .

nsects That Like to Party!

In terms of raw numbers, the world's most successful insects have got to be the social insects. These include bees, wasps, termites, and ants. It's a little-known fact that these insects invented social media by creating a buzz and chirping all the time.

Social insects such as ants and these Africanized bees are some of the world's most successful organisms.

Social insects live in large groups, or colonies, and work together to survive. Usually a colony is divided into a queen and workers. The queen lays the eggs. Workers hunt, feed the queen, defend the colony, build the nests, take care of the young, and vacuum the living room twice a day.

This system has made social insects the most dominant insects on Earth—and therefore the most dominant animals. One scientist estimated that for every human being on our planet, there are two hundred thousand ants—more than twice the number of football fans attending a typical Super Bowl championship game!

To give you a better idea of just how amazing social insects are, let me tell you a story.

Somewhere in Costa Rica...

A few years ago, I was backpacking through a lowland rainforest when all of a sudden I heard a strange sound. I looked down to see a thick column of black ants crossing my trail. Even more amazing, the ants were singing a song:

"We like to party!

We like to dance!

We like to party,

because we're ants!"

Well, maybe I was just *imagining* the singing part, but there were so many ants that I really could hear the scratching noise of thousands of ant feet scurrying across the leaves of the forest floor. They were army ants on the march.

Army ants live in colonies containing up to seven hundred thousand ants. They get their name from the way they hunt. Every morning the colony heads

Army ants maraud through tropical forests devouring almost anything in their wake.

out in one direction. The ants attack and kill every animal they come across, including tarantulas, scorpions, beetles, cockroaches, grasshoppers, and the adults and broods of other ants! As the army ants push forward, many animals attempt to flee. Those that cannot escape are killed and carried back to the main group.

For several weeks, army ants move to a new camp each day. Then they bivouac, or camp, so their queen can lay a new crop of eggs. Over a period of a few days, the queen lays between one hundred thousand and three hundred thousand eggs. As soon as the babies have hatched, the colony resumes its march to a new location, carrying the new generation of larvae with them.

In case you think that all social insects are mindless killing machines, I should point out that honeybees are also social insects. Of the world's twenty thousand or so species of bees, only a handful are honeybees, and only two or three of these have been harnessed by humans.

The common honeybee was brought to the Americas from Europe. It is a fairly mellow animal that will sting only when bothered or threatened. Beekeepers keep honeybees in large colonies of about sixty thousand each, and the bees work together to survive. Workers head out each day to gather pollen and nectar. Back at the hive, these raw materials are turned into honey and "bee bread" to feed the adults and larvae. Beekeepers manage the hives to produce honey. As the bees gather pollen, they also fertilize hundreds of different crops, from fruit trees to squash, peas, and other vegetables.

Colony Collapse Disorder—A Buzz Killer

In the last few years, honeybee hives have been dying in large numbers. Scientists have dubbed this Colony Collapse Disorder. No one is sure what causes CCD, but it may include a combination of pesticides, parasites, diseases, and climate change. Whatever is causing it, the impact on humans could be huge. Bees pollinate most of the crops that we eat, so a lot is riding on keeping the colonies healthy. Bees are so important that in 2015, President Obama ordered the creation of a special task force to figure out how to help bees and beekeepers. Even the leader of the free world wants to make sure honeybees party on.

Bees perform a vital service on our planet by pollinating most flowering plants.

As important as bees, ants, and other social insects are to the planet, there is one group of insects that rivals them as Rulers of the Known Universe. It's time to take a look at . . .

eetles—Masters of the Universe

Okay, I have to take a deep breath here, because beetles . . . beetles are *da bomb*! I've been going on and on about how many insect species there are and how amazing they are, right? Well, when it comes to beetles, multiply everything I've said by ten. Maybe by a hundred.

Beetles make up about 40 percent of all known insect species. So far, scientists have described about four hundred thousand different kinds. How many more are there? Some guess one hundred million. A more realistic guess is probably one to five million. Put in other terms, if you lined up all the known species of life on Earth, one out of every four of them would be a beetle! Is it any wonder that the most popular rock group ever named themselves after this group of insects—even if they couldn't spell it?

Why are there so many beetle species?

Scientists have several ideas about that. One is that many groups of beetles are able to feed on flowering plants. Flowering plants are almost everywhere on Earth, and there are a lot of different kinds. This has allowed beetles to evolve into a wide variety of species that have come up with many different ways to use and feed on the plants.

One of every four living species on Earth is a beetle.

Scientists also believe that the beetles' compact shape has helped them—literally—squeeze into a lot of different living spaces that other animals haven't been able to occupy.

The major key to beetle success, however, may lie in their hard wing coverings. These coverings are called elytra, and are actually the modified front wings of the insect. You'll find them on almost every beetle. Elytra do not help with flying—only the hind wings do that. Instead, elytra are armor that make beetles hard to kill. They also help keep beetles from drying out and, in some cases, protect the animals from overheating. For the 284 million years beetles have been on Earth, elytra have helped keep these insects from facing extinction. Meteors? Comets? Global warming? Beetles say, "Bring 'em on!"

Fireflies are beetles that use their bioluminescence to communicate.

Three beetle families have also evolved to be bioluminescent, which means they make their own light. The most famous bioluminescent beetles are fireflies. More than two thousand firefly species light up the night. You're likely to find them in any place that is warm and wet. One of the grooviest things I ever saw was in Malaysia, where an entire riverbank flashed on and off as tens of thousands of fireflies lit up at the same time.

Fireflies light up because they're afraid of the dark. Not really! Actually, male fireflies fly around while flashing light in order to attract females. The female usually sits on the ground or perches on a leaf, watching this display. If a male catches her fancy, she flashes back at him. The male lands and, if all goes well, they mate. Different firefly species flash unique signals to communicate, but males have to be careful. Some females flash to attract males of *different* species—only to eat them when they land!

Fireflies aren't the only bioluminescent beetles. Larval and adult female glowworms, or railroad worms, have pairs of light organs up and down their bodies. These animals search the soil and leaf litter for centipedes and other invertebrates to eat.

A few years ago I was hiking through a Costa Rican cloud forest when I encountered a third kind of bioluminescent beetle—a click beetle. There are more than 9,300 kinds of click beetles, and they live in most parts of the world. They get their name from the ability to "snap" part of their thoraxes. This action flings the beetle up into the air—startling a predator or helping to turn over the beetle when it ends up on its back. Some click beetles, though, have two little "headlights" on their thorax and another light organ on the first segment of their abdomen.

Like fireflies and glowworms, click beetles generate their light with a chemical called luciferin. The color of insect lights ranges from yellow to green to orange. One kind of glowworm even has a red light. While fireflies use their lights mostly in mating, click beetles and glowworms are thought to use lights to attract prey. More scientific studies are needed to *illuminate* their exact use.

Bombs Away

Beetles really are "da bomb." Especially bombardier beetles. They release combinations of chemicals that can explode in an attacker's face! The chemicals are produced inside the bombardier beetle's abdomen. When a beetle is threatened by another animal, the chemicals combine to produce temperatures of over two hundred degrees Fahrenheit. This creates a pressure that forces out a searing liquid, which the beetle can direct almost anywhere it wants. The chemical reaction is so violent and hot that it can kill some insect attackers— and scald a scientist's hand.

I encountered this bioluminescent click beetle while hiking through a Costa Rican cloud forest.

The Good, the Bad, and the Essential

By this point you've learned:

- Insects are amazing.
- Insects are everywhere.
- Insects are important to many different kinds of animals.

But there's one more thing you should know. Insects are also incredibly important to humans.

The Good

Insects offer enormous benefits to humans. In addition to providing us with honey, bees provide billions of dollars' worth of services to us by pollinating most of our fruit and vegetable crops. Insects prey on other insects, keeping many species from overrunning us or spreading disease. Dung beetles recycle billions of tons of poop every year—waste that would quickly turn our planet into one giant dung heap if beetles weren't "on the ball." Insects do other cool things for us as well.

- Cochineal insects provide red dyes for our clothes and food.
- Grasshoppers, grubs, termites, and other insects serve as food for people in many parts of the world.
- Insects such as fruit flies are often used to test new drugs.
- Beetles, butterflies, and other insects inspire legions of artists, poets, and writers.
- Some insect chemicals are even being investigated as possible medicines.

40

But, of course, with so many insects in the world, not all of them are going to become our BFFs—Bug Friends Forever.

The Bad

Have you ever noticed how Darth Vader from *Star Wars* looks a lot like an insect? That's no accident. People have developed a huge prejudice against insects over the years. That's probably because a few of them are rather villainous. Aphids attack our crops. Beetles and true bugs kill vast tracts of forests. Mosquitoes, lice, fleas, and flies bite us and, in the process, spread deadly diseases.

Although bees help us, other social insects can cause a lot of harm. Fire ants sting thousands of people every year, kill many native animals, and damage farm equipment. In the United States alone, fifty different species of wood-eating termites cause between $11 billion and $30 billion worth of damage to crops, homes, and other structures on an annual basis. Every year new invasive insect pests arrive on our shores and wreak havoc among us. A lot of this is our own fault, because we accidentally carry these animals to their new homes in our cars, planes, ships, and trains.

With their aggressive behavior and painful stings, fire ants rarely end up at the top of anyone's "Favorite Insects" list.

41

Scientists have only begun to identify and describe the millions of insects living in tropical forests. If that really bugs you, become an entomologist!

The Essential

Good or bad, ugly or beautiful, insects play a vital role on our planet. Unfortunately, what we don't know about insects far outweighs what we have learned. Scientists still haven't described—or even discovered—the vast majority of insects. Many insect species live high in the canopies of tropical forests, where the chances of finding them are small. To get a better idea of just how many insect and similar species actually live in tropical forests, one group of scientists recently spent thousands of hours catching, counting, and identifying insects, spiders, centipedes, and similar animals. In a single acre of rainforest, they collected 3,216 beetle species alone! And it will be decades—perhaps centuries—before we even begin to understand most of these animals.

So if you're wondering what to do with the rest of your life, may I suggest a career in entomology—the study of insects? The world needs people like you to study and learn about Earth's most abundant and dominant critters. Who knows what you will discover? A beetle that produces its own anti-cancer drug? An ant that controls weeds? A dragonfly that glows? One thing is guaranteed: you will never run out of insects to investigate!

Even if you don't choose entomology as a career, I hope this book has shown you that it's important for us all to continue . . .

Doing Right by Insects

I am not a fan of keeping insects as pets. I know it might seem cool to have a Madagascar hissing cockroach or a praying mantis, but most insect pets end up dying from neglect. Others escape to cause problems in places where they don't belong. A much better way of observing insects is to plant your own insect garden. It's easy to do. Just call your local agricultural extension service or visit a native-plant nursery to find out the names of some native flowering plants in your area. Buy a few seeds or plants and stick them in a small patch of ground. Make sure the plants get enough water. Then sit back and watch what happens. You will be amazed at the variety of butterflies, moths, beetles, bugs, and other insects that show up. Birds and spiders, too.

By putting a few native plants in the ground, you can be assured that you are helping insects, not hurting them. The greatest threat to insects today is the loss of their natural homes. Every time an acre of rainforest gets cut or burned, chances are that a few kinds of insects are going extinct forever. If you'd like to do even more than planting your own insect garden, consider joining a group that protects forests and other insect habitats. Here are a few that specialize in protecting tropical forests—where most insect species live:

A great way to help out your local insects is to grow a native plant garden.

You can often encounter cool insects just by walking down the street!

🐜 Amazon Conservation Association
   www.amazonconservation.org

🐜 Rainforest Alliance
   www.rainforest-alliance.org

🐜 Rainforest Trust
   www.rainforesttrust.org

🐜 Rainforest Foundation US
   www.rainforestfoundation.org

These molting cicadas are just some of the many fascinating insects you might encounter if you only go outside and look around.

Learning More—The Final Molt

Okay, at this point, I'm supposed to list books and websites for you to look at to learn more about insects. But guess what? I'm not gonna do it. You are all smart. You know how to go to the library, ask a teacher or librarian for book suggestions, or jump on the computer to learn more about insects from reputable websites. Besides poring over insect books and websites, what I *really* want you to do is to get your little insect-loving selves outside and watch these critters in person. Remember, insects *rule the world*. Unless it's twenty degrees below zero outside, you should have no trouble finding ants, butterflies, beetles, bees, and other insects to observe. So what are you waiting for? Go outside, find yourself an insect, and sit down to watch it. Bring a camera or a sketchpad or a journal with you. You'll learn something cool, and the best part is, you will do this using your own observation skills. You'll start to understand firsthand how all of us—humans and insects alike—fit into this amazing planet we call home.

hat's in a Name?

In this book I've mostly used common names to refer to insects. I don't mean names like "Fred" and "Matilda" and "José." Common names are names like "grasshoppers" and "ladybird beetles" and "butterflies"—names that everyone has heard. Scientists, though, have scientific names for groups of insects. These are usually based on the Greek language, and it's a lot of fun to learn them and know what they mean. At right are scientific names for orders of insects you're likely to encounter. After each name is a pronunciation guide, an explanation of what the scientific name means, and the common names for the animals in that group. You'll see that most of them include the root word "ptera," which is the Greek word for "wing." Scientists frequently change or "reshuffle" insect relationships. Don't be surprised to see some of these insects listed in different orders in other books and articles. Scientists will continue to change insect groups as they learn more—and agree or disagree about insect groupings.

It's not hard to figure out how these processionary caterpillars got their common name. Scientists also give insects scientific names based on Latin and Greek words.

Blattodea (BLAH-tow-DEE-uh), Latin for "cockroach" (big help, huh?): cockroaches, termites, and "water bugs"

Coleoptera (KOLE-ee-OP-tare-uh), "sheath-winged" insects: beetles

Diptera (DIP-tare-uh), "two-winged" insects: true flies, mosquitoes, and gnats

Hemiptera (hem-IP-tare-uh), "half-winged" insects: true bugs

Hymenoptera (HYE-men-OP-tare-uh), "membrane-winged" insects: ants, wasps, and bees

Isoptera (eye-SOP-tare-uh), insects with "equal-sized-wings" (sometimes combined with cockroaches in Blattodea or in a "superorder" called Dictyoptera)

Lepidoptera (LEH-pih-DOP-tare-uh), "scaly-winged" insects: moths and butterflies

Mantodea (MAN-tow-DAY-uh), "mantids": praying mantises

Odonata (OH-duh-NOT-uh), "toothed" insects: dragonflies and damselflies

Orthoptera (or-THOP-tare-uh), "straight-winged" insects: grasshoppers, crickets, locusts, and katydids

Phasmotodea (FAZ-mah-tow-DAY-uh), "phantom" insects: walking sticks

Glossary

(with definitions specific to insect species)

abdomen—an insect's hind section, which contains most internal organs and is often divided into seven to eleven segments

antennae (singular: antenna)—thin sensory organs that are attached to an insect's head; antennae can sense temperature, smell, touch, movement, sound, chemicals, and direction

bee bread—a mixture of pollen, honey, and bee saliva that is used as a source of food, especially for a hive's larvae

bioluminescence—the emission of light from living things

bivouac—to make temporary camp or a shelter

camouflage—colorations and patterns that help an insect blend into its background, protecting the insect from attack

chitin—the hard substance that makes up an insect's exoskeleton

circulatory system—a body system that pumps and carries blood through an animal's body and usually consists of a heart, blood, and blood vessels

cochineal insect—a type of scale insect that lives on cactus and is harvested to make brilliant red dye

colony—a large group of individuals living and working together

Colony Collapse Disorder—the failure or death of honeybee colonies; no one is sure what causes CCD, but it may include a combination of pesticides, parasites, diseases, and climate change

compound eye—an eye composed of many smaller units called ommatidia

digestive system—a body system that processes and absorbs food in order to provide an animal with energy

elytra (singular: elytron)—modified forewings of beetles; they protect the back wings and do not function in flight

entomology—the scientific study of insects

exoskeleton—the tough shell of an insect

invasive species—living organisms that travel or are taken to a new ecosystem where they cause harm

labium—the lower part of the mouth, often made from fused maxillae and used mostly to manipulate food; in honeybees, the labium is modified into a sucking tube

larva—the young or juvenile stage of an animal that often does not resemble its parents at the time it hatches or is birthed

luciferin—a chemical that helps produce light in bioluminescent organisms

mandibles—the part of an insect's mouth used in defense or to slice, tear, and crush food; typically the largest part of the mouth

maxillae (singular: maxilla)—mouthparts that manipulate food, located beneath the mandibles

metamorphosis—a transformation that takes place during the final larval stage, during which a juvenile animal turns into an adult

mimicry—the activity of one animal copying the behavior or look of another animal or object in order to hide from predators or lure unsuspecting prey

molt—to shed an old exoskeleton, allowing growth or further metamorphosis

nervous system—an animal's system of nerves that sends messages to and from the brain to control movement and feeling

ommatidia (singular: ommatidium)—the small units that make up a compound eye

parasitic—characterized by surviving through feeding off the tissues or blood of another living organism

parthenogenesis—reproduction that occurs when an egg is able to develop without being fertilized

pheromone—a chemical substance released by an organism that influences or affects other members of its species

plague—a large number of harmful things or a widespread problem or disease

pollinate—to transfer (male) pollen to the female part of a flower to achieve fertilization

pupa—the immobile, non-feeding stage of an insect during which it is changing from a juvenile to an adult form through the process of metamorphosis

reproductive system—the organs that work together to allow organisms to mate and make offspring

respiratory system—a set of organs that allows an animal to breathe and exchange oxygen and carbon dioxide throughout its body

serotonin—a naturally occurring chemical in the brain that helps regulate brain functions such as mood, appetite, sleep, and memory

social insects—animals that cooperate together in large colonies, such as ants, termites, bees, and wasps

spermatophore—a capsule or mass made by male insects that contains the male's sperm and is needed to reproduce with a female

spiracles—openings on an insect's exoskeleton that allow air into the body

stridulation—the process in certain insects of rubbing hard body parts together to make noise

thorax—the middle section of an insect, where wings and legs are attached

tracheae (singular: trachea)—the tubes or channels inside an insect's body that carry air to organs and tissues

ultraviolet light—wavelengths of light that are invisible to the human eye and assist some insects with navigation

venom—poison that is injected by one animal into another, with the intention of killing or injuring it

Index